Time Management

Developing Critical Routines, Optimizing Efficiency, And Leveraging The Potential Of Your Tailored Planner

(Developing Proficient Time Management Skills For Optimal Productivity And Well-Being)

Charlie Downey

TABLE OF CONTENT

Honour Yourself—You Deserve It! 1

The Secret To Success Is Discipline 15

Prioritising: Putting Tasks And Objectives In Order For Efficient Time Management 27

The Most Purely Impure Word 52

Determine Your Assignments 72

Time-Management Strategies 88

Effective Time Management And Psychological Well-Being 110

Divide Up The Work Into Doable Parts 133

Honour Yourself—You Deserve It!

Every time your child accomplishes anything exceptional, it's worth celebrating. Acknowledging their achievements with pride is essential for their motivation and self-worth.

But it's also critical to acknowledge and be proud of your accomplishments as a single mother.

Your path as a single mother is paved with setbacks and victories. It's critical to recognise and rejoice in these accomplishments, no matter how tiny. This is why it matters:

● Increasing self-confidence: Reminding yourself of your abilities and celebrating your achievements will help you feel more confident. It serves as a strong incentive to keep going.

● Setting a good example: You may teach your kids the value of self-worth and self-appreciation by acknowledging and celebrating your accomplishments. You serve as an example of positive self-esteem.

● Acknowledging patience: Your resilience is demonstrated by your ability to handle the challenges of being a single parent. Honouring your path demonstrates your resilience and strength.

● Promoting an optimistic atmosphere: Festivities in your house produce an optimistic and upbeat attitude. They provide opportunities for happiness, camaraderie, and introspection on your accomplishments.

You can commemorate your own and your kids' accomplishments in several ways, some of which are included below:

- Positive reinforcement: Use positive reinforcement to congratulate your youngster on their achievements. Honour their efforts and draw attention to their development.

- Personal milestones: Assign specific goals for yourself and your child. Celebrate these accomplishments with one another when they are reached. It might be finishing a task, getting a good grade, or getting beyond a difficulty.

- Family festivities: Plan unique family get-togethers to commemorate noteworthy accomplishments. These get-togethers foster lifelong memories and emphasise the value of community.

● Self-care routines: Celebrate yourself by indulging in self-care rituals. This could be treating yourself to a favourite dish, a spa day, or a beloved pastime.

● Expression of gratitude: Thank you for the experience and the advancements you've achieved. Keep a gratitude notebook to help you remember the good things in your life.

Honouring accomplishments—your own or your child's—helps to create a supportive and caring atmosphere. It builds resilience, self-worth, and a feeling of achievement.

Furthermore, it supports the notion that success involves acknowledging the work and progress made along the route in addition to the final objective.

Celebrating your accomplishments as a single mother is a great way to improve your self-worth, set an example of good behaviour for your kids, and foster a loving atmosphere at home. It's a confirmation that your efforts are impacting and acknowledging how far along you've come in life.

Thus, rejoice, feel pleased with yourself, and keep going forward with assurance and optimism.

Give up trying to be flawless.

The pursuit of perfection can be emotionally and mentally draining. Therefore, single mothers must let go of it. Being a single parent frequently entails many duties and difficulties, and attempting to uphold an unattainable standard of perfection simply causes needless strain and worry.

When they accept their shortcomings, single mothers may concentrate on what matters—giving their kids love, support, and a loving environment. It also promotes self-compassion by letting them realise that, despite the demands of their work, they are trying their best. Furthermore, recognising flaws can teach kids resilience and the value of accepting themselves—two important life lessons. Essentially, realising that it's acceptable to be flawed gives single mothers the confidence to put their happiness and their kids' happiness above impossible expectations, which eventually results in a more contented and balanced family life.

Seek motivation to support your path as a single mother.

Being a single parent can be challenging and complex, leaving many wondering how to be a successful single mother.

It's important to remember that you are not the only one going through these difficulties. There are many positive examples of accomplished single parents who have raised outstanding kids and made outstanding accomplishments.

Take the legacies of former Presidents Obama and Clinton, raised by single parents, as an example. Their experiences remind you that you are not alone in facing and overcoming comparable challenges.

You can also get ideas from the people in your social circle. Maybe you have a buddy who has succeeded as a single parent and can be a reliable confidant with insightful counsel and support. Connecting with these people can provide you with support and a feeling of community while you deal with the difficulties of being a single parent.

It's important to maintain your resolve and not give up on single parenthood—especially on those difficult days when it seems too much to bear.

Even if the road could be difficult, it's also a fantastic chance to raise and develop a remarkable human being.

Accept the encouragement of your loved ones and the examples of successful single parents as sources of motivation to help you along this amazing and fulfilling journey.

Recall that you are not just enduring your role as a single mother but thriving in it.

How to use the time slot technique

For several individuals, time is a limited and valuable asset. It can be hard to figure out how to maximise it. Using the time slot method, a time management strategy is one way to solve the problem. This strategy can increase your efficiency and production by dividing your day into "slots" or time. But in what practical sense is it used? Here, we walk you through it step-by-step.

Step 1: Determining the duties and undertakings

Make a list of all you have to get done during the day. These could be professional duties like meetings or projects, private pursuits like working out or shopping, or just downtime for rest.

Step 2: Calculating how much time will be needed

Next, determine an approximate time frame for each task or activity. At first, this could be challenging, particularly if you're not used to measuring your time in tasks. However, you will get more accurate at making these guesses as you become accustomed to doing so.

Step 3: Establishing the Schedules

It's time to schedule your day into time slots now that you have a list of chores and an estimate of the time you need each. You can use a paper calendar, a real calendar, or a digital calendar app to accomplish this. Allocate specific time slots for every work, allowing any required downtime or leisure time.

Step 4: Allocating assignments to time windows

After establishing your time slots, designate a specific slot for every task or activity. When doing this, try to be realistic and adaptable. If you know that your energy and productivity are at their peak in the morning, for instance, plan your most taxing duties now.

Step 5: Adhere to your plan

Maintaining focus is one of the hardest parts of the time slot technique. Interruptions are inevitable in life because they may be so unpredictable. But make every effort to adhere to your schedule. Do not worry if you stray. Simply restart and carry on.

Step 6: Examine and Modify

Lastly, take a minute to go over your schedule at the end of the day or week. Have you continued on your course? Have you overestimated or underestimated the amount of time required for particular tasks? Utilise this information to modify your plans for the future.

It is also crucial to note that while the time slot technique has used, it is not a panacea. It may take some time, just like any time management technique. You might need to modify it to fit your requirements as you become acclimated to it.

With time, you could discover that while certain jobs can be finished more quickly, others take longer than anticipated. Effective time management requires flexibility. If things don't go as planned, try not to become upset. Recall that the purpose of time management is to assist you in using your time more wisely and effectively rather than establishing a rigid schedule.

To be genuinely effective, though, it needs dedication, repetition, and ongoing refinement, just like any other method. With any luck, this book will assist you in putting this method into practice and getting time management.

The Secret To Success Is Discipline

Introduction

Teaching oneself to obey rules and uphold moral principles is a disciplined practice. It comprises setting goals, creating plans, and acting to achieve them. It necessitates self-control, self-regulation, and the ability to resist temptations and postpone enjoyment. Discipline may be advantageous in several areas of life, such as the workplace, school, athletics, and interpersonal relationships. It is an essential element for success and self-improvement.

It is the discipline of training oneself to obey authority figures and uphold moral standards. It comprises setting goals, creating plans, and acting to achieve them. It necessitates self-control, self-regulation, and the ability to resist temptations and postpone enjoyment. Discipline may be advantageous in several areas of life, such as the workplace, school, athletics, and interpersonal relationships. It is an essential element for success and self-improvement.

Put another way, while discipline is a concept everyone can grasp, not many people value it.

Even the most well-known historical personalities needed to maintain discipline. Without it, all living creatures would find themselves in a confused world. Discipline must be appreciated by everybody for its presence.

It is said that "life without order is like a ship without radar."

Students who follow the rules have a higher chance of being fortunate and succeeding in all facets of their lives.

Thus, it is difficult to undervalue student life and discipline's importance.

You need to have steadfast patience if you want to be a strong and inspirational leader. It's brave to refuse.

Whatever you genuinely enjoy. Your greatest decisions in life have the power to create or destroy you, and people like this one tend to do just that. Anytime you exhibit self-control, it will remind you how important discipline is to your quest for sustained success.

One's life gains structure and harmony via practice. It teaches people to respect others and accept responsibility for their conduct. The foundation of civilization is the observance of well-defined laws. Without a framework, people would act. However, they pleased and made mistakes without carefully considering their actions. It improves humanity and makes the world a more pleasant place to work and live, which makes it easier for us to do good deeds.

An individual who possesses the ability to self-regulate can function in an authentic, disciplined, and controlled manner. A lack of this ability could have disastrous results. Would a company hire someone who frequently arrives late for work or has a track record of missing deadlines? It is obvious how these actions could harm a company's reputation.

Using athletics as an example, all teams must follow the game's rules, and preparation is essential to success; because of this, arbitrators and arbitraries exist. If someone disobeys these rules, they will be held accountable for breaking the sport's rules.

High performers must exercise the proper restraint; not only are they able to communicate, but they also exude confidence. Knowledgeable leaders know when to speak and when to be silent. It is advised to practise discipline and self-constitution to develop one's heart and mind.

There are two fields: the inside and the outside. The ability to distinguish between good and bad is known as internal consistency. External control centres on social norms such as law enforcement. It takes discipline to use exceptional gifts; having them is not enough.

People will usually experience immediate satisfaction. People in positions of power cannot look into the long-term effects of their choices. This shows how vital this skill is for survival and suggests that it may be the most important component in reaching an objective. You can achieve the outcomes you want by carefully selecting from various options. It also gives you the fortitude to overcome obstacles.

You can focus on this talent anytime to help it grow or improve. Just promise to uphold your half of the agreement.

Strive to keep your emotions, behaviours, and attitudes in check. Training can be done on the mental and physical levels.

By emphasizing the positive qualities above all else, you might be able to avoid sending the wrong signals.

The rationale behind school discipline

One of the most crucial aspects of a student's life is discipline. Since discipline is essential for success in life, it is something that students must learn. In the classroom, student discipline is crucial.

The Secret to Success is Discipline

The degree of success and satisfaction in life may greatly impact their discipline. It is the ability to control one's actions and impulses while adhering to rules or principles. Apart from accomplishing individual goals, self-control is necessary to maintain interpersonal connections, thrive in the workplace, and lead a fulfilling life.

One of the main reasons discipline is essential in life is the capacity to set and achieve goals. It's easy to become sidetracked and forget what matters most when you lack self-control. Disciplined people may take the necessary steps to achieve their goals while staying motivated and focused. This holds irrespective of the goal's connection to relationships, employment, health, or personal development.

Discipline is important in life because it helps people develop the ability to control themselves. This skill is necessary to succeed and enjoy life. People who possess discipline can regulate their impulses and resist temptations that could otherwise have negative consequences.

Discipline is also crucial in partnerships. Relationship maintenance requires some commitment and effort. Ignoring and taking other people's needs for granted is easy when one lacks discipline. Disciplined people can communicate more effectively, prioritize the needs of others, and accept accountability for their actions. This is true whether the relationship is with a friend, family member, or romantic partner.

Maintaining discipline in the workplace is essential for success and career advancement. Employers place great importance on workers who can meet deadlines, are dependable, and show up on time. Disciplined people can operate efficiently, produce results, and handle the pressure of meeting deadlines and expectations at work. Employees who do this stand out more at work and have a better chance of getting promoted or given a raise.

Ultimately, discipline is important since it leads to a sense of fulfilment and contentment in life. Individuals who can set and achieve goals, exercise self-control, uphold positive relationships, and succeed in their occupations are more likely to lead meaningful lives. Discipline is not always easy, but the rewards make the effort worthwhile.

To sum up, discipline is an essential life attribute that can greatly impact someone's happiness and success. It allows people to set and achieve goals, develop self-control, maintain positive relationships, and excel at work.

Discipline can lead to pleasant, fulfilling lives for people.

Prioritising: Putting Tasks And Objectives In Order For Efficient Time Management

First of all,

The key to efficient time management is the capacity to rank objectives and tasks. This chapter explores the skill of prioritizing tasks and planning activities to guarantee efficient use of time. Readers may increase productivity and feel more accomplished by making well-informed decisions about spending their time and energy by grasping the principles of prioritization.

The Value of Establishing Priorities

Navigating the many duties and obligations that occupy our lives requires setting priorities. The importance of prioritization and how it contributes to both professional and personal success are discussed in this section. The advantages of matching activities to broad objectives will be explained to readers, who will discover how establishing priorities may improve focus, lessen stress, and give work a feeling of direction.

Time Optimization: By setting priorities, people can more effectively manage their time and give important tasks the time and attention required.

Goal Achievement: The probability of achieving objectives and milestones increases when actions align with particular goals.

Stress Reduction: By offering an organized method for managing obligations, well-defined priorities aid in reducing overwhelm and stress.

Prioritization enables people to concentrate on important tasks, which fosters deeper concentration and higher-quality work.

Setting priorities aids in resource management by directing time, effort, and attention towards the tasks that impact achievement most.

Better Decision-Making: A clear framework for assessing opportunities and selecting the most pertinent helps with decision-making.

Increased Time Awareness: Setting priorities helps people become more conscious of how much time they spend on various tasks, promoting more thoughtful time management.

Determine High-Priority Objectives and Tasks:

In-depth methods for determining high-priority tasks and objectives are covered in this section. The ability to distinguish between significant and urgent tasks, as well as how to match activities to long-term goals, will be imparted to readers. We'll examine methods for determining priorities over the short and long terms, enabling readers to design a successful road map.

Eisenhower Matrix: Using the matrix to classify tasks, comprehend the idea of urgency vs importance.

SMART goals are specific, measurable, attainable, relevant, and time-bound aims. They are created by applying these criteria to the formulation of objectives.

Cost-benefit analysis is the process of ranking tasks according to their possible costs and benefits.

Aligning with Core Values: Select activities that enhance a sense of fulfilment and are consistent with one's or the organization's core values.

Time constraints: Setting deadlines and time-sensitive obligations for projects.

Effect on Other Goals: Determining how the accomplishment of a certain task will affect the advancement of other goals.

Setting Up Objectives and Tasks:

After determining priorities, this section looks at methods for setting structured tasks and objectives. The skills of making useful to-do lists, deadlines, and time management will be imparted to readers. We'll also talk about how to use technology, including task management applications and digital calendars, to set priorities.

Making use of contemporary instruments to improve your output

Using Contemporary Tools to Increase Productivity

Maintaining productivity in the ever-changing modern environment is a daily struggle. Thank goodness technology has provided us with many tools and methods to increase productivity and enable us to complete tasks faster. Let's explore how you can use these innovative technologies to increase output and accomplish your goals.

Chatbots: Your Virtual Companions

Our relationship with technology has changed significantly due to smart assistants like Google Assistant, Amazon's Alexa, and Apple's Siri. These voice-activated virtual assistants allow you to send messages, schedule reminders, and even operate smart home appliances. They enable us to complete jobs more quickly because they integrate smoothly with our daily lives.

Task Management Applications: Skillful Scheduling

An electronic centre for your to-do lists can be found with task management applications like TickTick, Todoist, and Wunderlist (Microsoft To Do). You can ensure nothing is missed by classifying tasks, setting deadlines, and monitoring progress. With the help of these tools, you can efficiently prioritize tasks and keep your workflow organized.

Tools for Taking Notes: Digital Idea Capturing

The days of writing notes on paper are long gone. Digital applications such as Evernote, Microsoft OneNote, and Bear allow you to digitally collect and arrange ideas. Organize your ideas into notebooks for various tasks, label notes for quick access, and access them from any device anytime.

Apps that Improve Focus: Overcoming Distractions

Focus-enhancing apps are helpful in a world where there are a lot of digital distractions. You may improve your concentration by creating dedicated work periods and eliminating distracting websites.

Software for Tracking Time: Gain Visibility Into Your Day

Time-tracking applications such as Harvest, Clockify, and Toggl provide insight into your daily routine. By classifying tasks and generating reports, these applications assist you in locating time wasters and potential areas for improvement. This information allows you to adapt your habits and manage your time effectively.

Automation Options: Optimized Processes

Automation solutions that connect apps and automate processes, like Zapier and Integromat, function as digital assistants.

For example, you can create a routine to post changes to social media on many platforms at once or automatically store email attachments in cloud storage. These instruments spare you from laborious manual tasks.

Online Gatherings: An International Link

Google Meet has completely transformed communication and cooperation. They make it easy to run seminars, webinars, and meetings and promote real-time communication between people in different places.

Cloud Storage: Accessible From Any Location

Cloud storage options like Dropbox, Google Drive, and Microsoft OneDrivelift physical storage limitations. You may work in real time with team members, view your files from anywhere, and protect your data with automated backups.

Apps for Learning Languages: Educating on the Go

You can maximize downtime with the help of apps for learning languages, such as Duolingo, Babbel, and Rosetta Stone. In short bursts, you can pick up a new language for your commute or vacation. Over time, this effective use of free time can result in a large increase in competence.

Tools for Financial Management: Streamlining Budgeting

Financial management is made easier by apps like PocketGuard and Mint, which combine your accounts and classify spending. Without the trouble of manual computation, they assist you in setting financial objectives, monitoring your expenditures, and creating budgets.

Audiobooks and Educational Podcasts: Learning on the Go

Invest your downtime in educational opportunities by listening to podcasts and audiobooks. While working out, travelling, or doing housework, you can learn new information, keep yourself updated, and expand your knowledge base.

Getting the Hang of Modern Tools: A Route to Greatness

Using these contemporary technologies in your daily routine can completely change your function in the digital world. But remember that these tools supplement conscious work practices—not their replacements.

Accept the world of opportunities technology presents, try various tools, and assemble a toolset that complements your goals. You may reach new heights of productivity and get closer to your goals by using technology wisely. Be curious, flexible, and prepared to modify your strategy as you hone your productivity toolkit.

Controlling Interruptions and Distractions

Distractions and interruptions are inevitable, no matter how reserved we try to be. But that doesn't mean we must abandon our actions to appease them every time. The birthday of a friend's dog can occasionally wait until the end of the workweek. Similarly, most texts allow for a delayed response with minimal consequences. But first, we need to identify our distractions to better control them.

The workplace has become increasingly globalized in tandem with society. This has several benefits, from our ability to collaborate with people from different backgrounds to the possibility of building a global network of friends and colleagues. On the other hand, communication is a major source of our frequent distractions. It's all too common in today's environment to have a well-intentioned call cut short during a meeting. Similarly, hearing incessant "blips" from a tab distant during spreadsheet filling has become a common source of headaches and pauses. Non-social distractions can also include cravings for leftover turkey from home, nervousness over an impending social engagement, and other things! One thing unites them all, though. They usually don't have much bearing on our actions and aren't urgent.

Consider for a moment the distractions that you observe at work. Remember not to categorize them as bad but rather as unsuitable. For instance, when I have a little time to myself, I like to have a cup of tea. I tried to keep a kettle and a few tea bags close at hand in my workspace for a while. Since I always had tea on hand, I hoped this would boost my motivation. This, however, backfired. Occasionally, I would lose an hour or two just making and drinking tea! After realizing how this hurt my productivity, I thought there had to be a better solution. I tried making tea in advance at home and taking a full thermos to work. I felt less restricted almost instantly. My logs for the next week confirmed what I felt: although I was still drinking my favourite beverage to stay hydrated, it was no longer taking up an eighth of my working hours.

Now that we've recognized a few typical distractions, we can decide when and how to address them. For instance, if your office has an open-door policy, this can be readily fixed. Rethink what it means to be accessible, and leave your door open or closed for a while. Make it obvious that entry does not guarantee you will have the time or resources to help with a specific task. Alec Mackenzie suggests creating a plan to have it accessible for guests in the same spirit. In this manner, a thirty-minute talk is condensed to a flowchart. Make sure you are succinct: Just share the required information and indicate to them that you have an important assignment to complete.

Let us address the unaddressed matter at hand: smartphones. Even though they use many contemporary features, research has indicated that actively using them can be highly distracting. Furthermore, studies have also been done on the negative effects of having a phone in your line of sight! We now know that having cell phones within visual range, even when not in use, hurts productivity (Thornton et al., 2014). You may want to try hiding your phone to combat this.

Additionally, you might want to consider setting up a time when all alerts are silenced. If your employer has given you a work phone, this is the easiest, but make a strategy and try out some other methods. For instance, you may use Telegram exclusively for business communications while using WhatsApp for personal messaging with your friends and family. Consequently, you might choose quiet times for the latter chat app while remaining informed of important work-related calls!

Establishing limits is also essential to a creative atmosphere. Grand gestures like this are unproductive and inefficient despite Hollywood's best efforts to persuade us otherwise. Imagine showing up at your loved one's office amid the workday with roses and a speech about owning up to your mistakes. Joking aside, communicate to loved ones what is and isn't appropriate during working hours. For example, there's nothing wrong with checking in during your lunch break. However, that is far different from them barging in without permission. Make it clear that you would rather maintain concentration during working hours.

But don't mistake setting boundaries for being aloof. Happier people are more productive, as we have already covered. Furthermore, being with our loved ones usually lifts our spirits because we are social beings. Rather, pay attention to the time you spend with the people you love. And pay attention to the here and now, just like I advise you to do at work. Be with them; don't just be close to them.

Boundaries also apply to your boss and fellow employees. Tell them the truth. If a supervisor attempts to overstep their authority—for example, by assigning more work when you already have many pressing matters on your plate or trying to violate your morals—you should politely inform them of this. If the problem goes beyond a drop in productivity, take advantage of the options available to help yourself. But knowing your team's timetable is just excellent practice for maximizing work output. But we'll go into more detail about that in a few chapters.

In a similar vein, our working environment has an impact on our output. Interestingly, there was no accepted definition of office comfort at the time, as suggested by Haynes (2008), who stated, "There is enough evidence to support the claim that office comfort can affect productivity." I hope we can take advantage of that. In addition to the obvious things like having a tidy desk and being in a well-lit space, play around with little details. Perhaps pack some water and make small activities out of drinking it. You may feel cosier because of this since you will be more hydrated!

Similarly, rearrange some of the furniture in your office if you have the room. I used to feel most at ease when coloured notes surrounded me. These chores filled a gradient from red ones that had to be completed within the day to pastel yellow ones that encouraged rest. Although crowded, it was tidy.

These Chapters have helped us understand ourselves better. Through journaling and meditation, we have actively engaged in reflection. We have set limits to keep exchanges between work and play separate. You've even mastered the art of doing away with procrastination! But we have to move on to scheduling now. This falls into our top-right quadrant of the Eisenhower Matrix, and if we work efficiently, it will eventually include most of what we do. Planning and wise time management are the keys to accomplishing more, as simple as it may sound! Together with discussing how to maintain motivation throughout and live a more balanced existence, I'll also offer some advice on assigning chores to maximize your time. Now, let's get going!

The Most Purely Impure Word

Establishment

SME Organisational Skills

Is your excessive workload a result of your inability to organise yourself? Effective organisational abilities are arguably the most overlooked characteristic of prosperous businesspeople. In the modern business world, executives must be able to efficiently handle and analyse the vast volume of information they are exposed to daily from many sources.

Both a business and personal level must be addressed regarding organisation. A business team's members must coordinate efficiently, plan, and focus on one or two main objectives. They must be good communicators, exchange schedules, and regularly update contact details for clients and themselves.

Workspace Workspaces must be set up so that all employees can easily access resources when needed. The entire office's productivity will suffer if just one individual forgets to refile crucial documents or puts them wherever they can be filed again. How recently did you tidy your virtual desktop? Most computer desktops are disorganised, with several file names, directories inside folders, and icons.

Due to password lack, production may stop when an employee is absent.

Maintain an up-to-date master password list somewhere accessible yet secure.

Procedure Structure

Processing mail is another area where an organisation might save time. As soon as the mail arrives, it should be opened and organised into three piles: advertising, checks that need to be deposited, and accounts payable. Handle each mail item once and work on one pile at a time. Allowing these heaps to grow makes it possible for you to speed through to catch up and miss something crucial. Keep in mind that you don't have to save every document that comes across your desk. It's common to find the same information elsewhere. For instance, bank data and magazine articles can now be found online.

You can intentionally set up your workstation on a personal level to increase productivity. Assume a central position within your workspace. Store big numbers of goods so they are out of the way, and just keep a small amount on hand. Every time you finish a task, tidy up. Don't let supplies accumulate. Store gear like printers and scanners on the tops of bookcases and filing cabinets. Thus, usable workspace will be freed up. Lastly, scan and store papers digitally. Always create a backup copy and discard paper copies.

You will only benefit from this filing strategy if your company's PCs are running a productive file management system.

10. Constantly Developing Better Time Management

Strategies and Methods for Continuous Improvement and Development.

Effective time management is an ongoing process of development. In this chapter, we'll look at several strategies for enhancing time management in your company over time.

1. Examine and assess

You have to examine and assess your existing time management methods before you can make continual improvements. This entails determining your advantages and disadvantages and any room for improvement. To do this, carry out routine time audits, evaluate team member performance, and ask team members for input.

2. Establish objectives and goals

A crucial element of ongoing improvement is goal-setting. You can concentrate on the areas where you need the most development by establishing specific goals and objectives. One way to do this is to set SMART goals—specific, measurable, realistic, relevant, and time-bound.

3. Put New Methods and Approaches into Practice

You must be open to trying different tactics and methods to consistently get better at managing your time. This could be implementing new time management software and tools, updating your policies and procedures, or giving your staff members more guidance and assistance.

4. Invite suggestions and comments

Encouraging team members' opinions and suggestions is crucial to ongoing development. You may find areas for improvement and make changes that will help the entire organisation by asking your team members for their opinions. Regular surveys, team gatherings, or one-on-one discussions with team members can all help achieve this.

5. Track Development and Honour Achievements

A critical component of continuous improvement is tracking advancement and acknowledging accomplishments. You can see how far you've gone and pinpoint areas where you still need to improve by keeping track of your progress. Honouring accomplishments can also be a strong source of inspiration for your group and provide impetus for further advancements.

6. Encourage an Environment of Constant Improvement

Lastly, you need to cultivate a continuous improvement culture in your company to keep improving time management. This entails empowering your team members to take responsibility for their time management techniques, offering chances for personal and professional advancement, and acknowledging accomplishments.

Actual Cases

Here are a few actual instances of how businesses have consistently enhanced their time management procedures:

- A consulting firm solicited team member feedback and introduced new project management tools to optimise workflow and boost productivity; a healthcare provider performed routine time audits and added new scheduling software to decrease wait times and increase patient satisfaction.

- A nonprofit organisation outlined specific aims and objectives for their fundraising campaigns and acknowledged team members who went above and beyond to celebrate accomplishments.

The Basics of Individual Growth

Personal Growth: What Is It?

Personal growth is known as becoming a better version of oneself in one's job, relationships, health, and general well-being. It includes a path devoted to realising and pursuing one's potential.

For those with intelligence, why is it valuable?

Knowledge is a thirst that intelligent people have, and they can efficiently satisfy this thirst with personal development. It allows people to grow, overcome obstacles, and achieve their goals.

The Advantages of Personal Growth: growth has benefits such as improved self-awareness, increased confidence, sharpened problem-solving skills, increased productivity, strengthened interpersonal relationships, and improved physical and mental health.

How to Begin Your Personal Development Journey:

There are various methods to start your road towards growth. Consider the following advice: ● Set goals: Determine your life's ambitions first. You may plan to accomplish your goals after you clearly grasp them.

Determine your advantages and disadvantages; Consider your strengths and opportunities for development. Knowing your strengths and areas for improvement allows you to concentrate on improving those areas.

● Look for someone who has already accomplished your goals to serve as a mentor or coach. They can offer assistance and direction as you progress through your growth.

Participate in workshops or courses; some resources provide opportunities to learn new skills and promote personal development.

- Read books and articles; delve into development-related material, which might offer insightful information.
- Act: Ultimately, the most important stage is to take action towards your objectives—making a start is essential.

In summary, having a happy and meaningful life is a function of personal development. It's critical to remember that progress is a continuous process rather than a destination, although paved with ups and downs.

Those who are intelligent frequently have an understanding of their talents and shortcomings. However, they could find it difficult to build on their areas of weakness or leverage their strengths.

Overcoming these obstacles can involve personal development and progress.

In addition, intelligent people could be driven to achieve. They might not know how to define objectives or build a thorough strategy. Development activities might provide direction in this area.

Furthermore, it's not unusual for intellectual people to hang around with other intelligent people. However, they can discover that they are not surrounded by people who can push them intellectually or help them along their path of personal development.

Chapter 8: Organise Yourself

Research on workplace stress states that forty per cent of workers consider their jobs extremely stressful. In a different study, the Attitudes in the American Workplace VII survey, sponsored by the Marlin Company and conducted by Harris Interactive in 2001, 33% of workers claimed their jobs negatively affected their physical and mental health; 42% claimed work pressures interfered with their relationships. Based on the results of this study, half of the workers reported that their workload had increased from the previous year, and almost the same number indicated they were overworked or faced excessive deadlines. Notably, 73% of respondents claimed they wouldn't want to be their boss. A 2006 Gallup poll found that at least 40% of full-time or part-time Americans report experiencing stress regularly. This research also revealed that 61 per cent of full-time workers feel they don't have enough time to accomplish everything on their to-do lists.

Unexpected demands from outside sources and challenging and relentless workloads can lead to stress and frustration. Our emotional state, level of productivity, and even our health may suffer as a result. Without question, these pressures have a big impact on our lives. If we could better manage our professional and personal responsibilities, we wouldn't feel this stress and be more vulnerable to its effects. Using an organisational system that logs our personal and professional tasks, describes their steps, helps us prioritise them, and helps us manage our lives more effectively.

Recognise the Reality

We have a tonne of work, from small and insignificant (like lubricating the squeaky bathroom door hinge) to large and significant. (finding a retirement community for Dad, putting together a significant presentation). All these chores are part of the nagging "undone" that occupy our conscious and unconscious brains, and while some may be more vital than others, Dad's health and pleasure should come before a noisy door. We periodically experience random thoughts and unfortunate occurrences—like remembering to stamp an envelope after mailing it—because we have limited control over our thinking. It also means that we will most likely be thinking about the impending presentation and how to correct that awful slice while we are playing golf or in the middle of a staff meeting. You'll also think about retirement communities and creaky hinges at strange times.

This massive mass of random thoughts will continue to spin because life moves too quickly for us to handle the ones that have already collided. What happens next? Unless you're living the rustic life of a secluded shepherd, you have to face the fact that there are numerous demands on your time, interruptions are unavoidable, and your career, family, friends, and community will continue to demand our attention in unexpected ways at inconvenient periods. During recess, your child will trip and break his wrist; he needs to be rushed straight away to the emergency room of the hospital. Your boss will stop by your office before lunch to ask you to investigate a contract and report back to her with the findings. A colleague will call with "just a few questions," but there's no way they can cover everything in a half-hour.

From the project's current status to yesterday's football match. These are the consequences of being alive. We can only pick our response to these situations; we can do nothing about them. You can implement strategies to manage disruptions and mitigate their impact, like answering calls through voicemail and removing the visitor chair from your workspace. Hence, visitors cannot sit down. Some techniques might be worthwhile, particularly if you believe others frequently try to take advantage of you. More than the reality that most people are just trying to get by, your insecurity is shown by the bad intent you attribute to others. Over time, dealing with disruptions when they arise and addressing them head-on is more practical. We can quickly become overwhelmed by events and lose our ability to function if we don't react logically.

Determine Your Assignments

Now that we know we probably have more work than we have time for and that new requests will arise before we have a chance to finish the old, we need to put a control mechanism in place. If not, fresh and unfinished work will accumulate and impede your progress. We must first be able to swiftly, painlessly, and readily capture our obligations to be able to control them. (For further advice on creating lists, go to Chapter 5, Use the To-Do List

Effectively.) For this, you can use sticky notes, index cards (which help shift objects if there are many), or a notebook. (helpful for quickly glancing at the overall picture). Alternatively, you might find that finishing this step in a word processor or spreadsheet file is more convenient. Choose the approach that works best for you to keep track of all your commitments and incomplete chores.

This stage will appear disorganised because all jobs should be recorded, not just the most critical ones, and because they shouldn't be completed in a specific order. Once you've completed every project for which you are responsible at work, allow your mind to stray to extracurricular pursuits and make an effort to jot down every task unrelated to your employment. Give a detailed description of everything; setting priorities is done later. To the best of your abilities, list your responsibilities as well as all duties related to any positions you may play, such as those of a partner or spouse, parent, child, sibling, friend, coworker, team member, homeowner, volunteer, supporter, adviser, contributor, etc. The recurring long-term obligations and the one-time, short-term tasks must be mentioned. How can "spending time with family" be put into words? It is possible to record your son's weekly lacrosse matches and your daughter's regular soccer practice.

Including the item "Spending time with family." is also an excellent idea, as it will force you to reflect more deeply and develop a plan of action to accomplish this goal. This is also an excellent time to schedule a weekly or bimonthly "date" with your partner or significant other.

The obvious responsibilities to your family that come with being a parent or spouse might not seem like they belong on your list. You declare that "I'm doing these things anyhow." Maybe you're the best spouse, father, or partner on two legs, and you don't want to put your time with your loved ones on the impersonal task list and treat it like a "task." Remember that you are setting up a method to ensure that the commitments on your list are fulfilled.

Creating this master list of chores, or super "to-do" list, in whatever format you choose will undoubtedly take a lot of work, but if you follow the instructions in the "schedule" section below, you may be able to skip this stage entirely. Unfortunately, a standard to-do list does not allow for understanding the work at hand, creating a plan for it, or identifying the resources—like time—that will be needed to finish it. Thus, both "Write a will" and "Oil the bathroom door" are equally crucial at this stage. That means your list is just as random and disjointed as your ignorant assumptions. The following steps will deal with that issue.

Describe

It's time to describe your unfinished business and outstanding responsibilities now that you have listed them all. This is a crucial phase to schedule, prioritise, and formulate an effective action plan. In this phase, you specify the actions that must be followed to finish the assignment and determine how long each one will take. Smaller jobs, like oiling the bathroom door hinge, are given less time because they only need to locate the oil, spray a few drops, and mop up any spilt oil on the floor. The entire task takes five minutes if you know where to find the oil and don't spill any on the carpet. No one will even notice if you do that on the way to dinner, apart from the fact that there won't be a squeak. The task will require more stages and take longer if you don't know where the oil is, don't have any, or are incredibly sloppy, and there's a white carpet behind that hinge. However, all these variables can be considered by following this definition step.

This definition stage is proportionately more important for larger assignments. The procedure can become close to project management complexity if your assignment involves persuading others to agree, money, contracts, the government, the weather, etc. This list can get lengthy because it allows the work at hand to make the defining stage essential for complex projects. In actuality, understanding the actions involved and the order in which they must be accomplished is only achievable by segmenting a huge work into smaller ones. In the defining stage, the impossibly difficult becomes feasible.

If you have a task like creating a report and dread it because you know it will take a lot of time and effort, defining the report's components will help you handle it much more easily. Writing an outline is still a terrific approach to organise your ideas, even if you were taught in school that it's the greatest way to prepare a report. You may also find that the mind mapping method works best for taking notes on concepts presented in other parts of this book. Devoting even thirty minutes to this organising phase will make you feel like you've progressed towards the ultimate goal.

Set priorities.

Prioritisation is essential to the process of structure and control. Priorities are those behaviours that impact your ability to achieve your goals; hence, setting goals is a prerequisite to selecting priorities. You must think long-term while establishing your goals to set long-term targets and consider personal and professional ambitions. Setting priorities is essential because there isn't enough time to complete your tasks.

Even while bigger projects will take longer to finish, this does not mean you should schedule or prioritise them for when you are at your "prime time." While smaller jobs can and should be completed quickly, they must be prioritised equally with larger ones.

Chapter 3: Breaking Time-Wasteful Habits

Everybody has time-consuming habits that don't enhance their lives. These time-wasting behaviours might first appear harmless or even pleasurable, but they have the potential to accumulate over time and rob valuable minutes from more worthwhile pursuits. Binge-watching TV series or aimlessly browsing social media feeds are two of the most popular time-wasting behaviours. Even though it could seem like a soothing method to wind down after a demanding day, it can easily become hours upon hours lost. Establish a daily screen time limit to overcome this bad habit. Aim to substitute some of your screen time with enjoyable pursuits such as hobbies.

Constantly checking your email or messages is another time-consuming behaviour you should eliminate. It's simple to become overwhelmed by the never-ending messages and believe that we must reply to everything right away. But doing so can start a vicious loop of interruptions and distractions that divert our attention from more crucial work. Rather, designate particular periods of the day to review and reply to communications. This will help you maintain your attention on the current task and prevent you from becoming distracted by outside distractions.

Another significant time-wasting behaviour that a lot of us deal with is procrastination. We procrastinate until the last minute, then rush to finish things while experiencing tension and feeling overwhelmed. Try assigning deadlines to each work and dividing them into smaller, more manageable steps to help you kick this habit. Hold yourself accountable if you use productivity software to monitor your progress or ask a friend for assistance.

Lastly, low-priority and busy work can take up a surprising amount of time without bringing us closer to our objectives. Even though these chores seem vital or urgent, they frequently divert our attention from more important activities. Make a list of your top priorities and concentrate on them first to help you avoid falling into this trap. To make more time for the things that matter, assign or remove low-priority activities whenever possible.

Recall that time is money and that each minute lost is one that we cannot get back. We may invest in our future and have more fulfilled lives by kicking these time-wasting habits and taking charge of our schedules.

It takes work to break time-wasting behaviours, but the effort is worthwhile. Every minute we lose to pointless pursuits is a minute we could have used to do something more worthwhile and satisfying. Everybody has time-wasting habits, whether it's endlessly scrolling through social media, binge-watching TV, or getting sucked into office gossip.

But we can regain control over our time and use it better if we recognise these behaviours and take action to break them. We can make time for the important things in life, like following our passions, spending time with our loved ones, or caring for ourselves.

The world's most successful individuals—business titans, athletes, and artists—all recognise time's importance. They are aware that each minute lost is one that they cannot get back. They make the most of every moment by setting priorities and managing their time well.

So, let's take a cue from them and stop wasting time. Let's take charge of our time, invest in the future, and lead happier, more meaningful lives. Time is money, but it's much more than that—it's our most valuable resource. Keep that in mind. Come to that sensible use.

Steer clear of

Procrastination frequently results in avoidance. We might skip the task or devise reasons for not finishing it. Avoidance has the potential to be dangerous since it might result in missed deadlines and lost opportunities. To overcome avoidance, it's critical to face the work head-on. Establish modest, doable objectives and acknowledge your advancements as you go.

Recall that time is money and that each minute lost is one that we cannot get back. We can take charge of our time and invest in our futures by overcoming avoidance and procrastination. We can combat procrastination and regain our time by tackling activities head-on, removing distractions, connecting tasks to larger goals, addressing self-doubt, and splitting tasks into smaller portions.

Section 2: Increasing Output

Time-Management Strategies

It takes planning, focus, and discipline to manage time well. This chapter'll look at various time management strategies to help us maximise our time, boost output, and accomplish our objectives.

The Pomodoro Technique: This method divides your workday into 25-minute halves and requires a 5-minute rest. You take a lengthier pause of 20 to

30 minutes after four intervals. You may prevent burnout and maintain focus by using this strategy, which divides your job into small, achievable tasks.

Using the Eisenhower Matrix, jobs are divided into four groups according to their urgency and significance. These fall into four categories: not important or urgent, not urgent but important, not urgent but important, and urgent but not important. Have the biggest influence on your objectives by ranking them according to significance and urgency.

Time blocking: This method entails setting aside time in blocks for designated jobs or endeavours. This aids in preventing distractions and maintaining your attention on one work at a time. It also guarantees that you allocate adequate time to significant assignments and undertakings.

The Ivy Lee Method: This method entails setting a daily priority list of six things to be completed and concentrating on finishing them before tackling other tasks. This keeps you focused on what matters most and prevents you from getting overwhelmed by a lengthy to-do list.

States that 20% of your efforts should yield 80% of your results. You may boost your productivity and do more work in less time by concentrating on the projects with the biggest impact.

Single-tasking: This method entails concentrating on a single task simultaneously, blocking out distractions. This can be especially useful for assignments that call for a high level of concentration and focus.

Timeboxing: This method gives a task or project a set amount of time and concentrates on doing it within the allotted period. This can be helpful for jobs that tend to become larger to fit the available time.

These methods are only a handful of the numerous time management strategies. It's crucial to try various methods to determine which suits you the most. Recall that time is money and that each minute lost is one that we cannot get back. By employing efficient time management strategies, we may maximise our time, boost output, and accomplish our objectives.

Chapter 3: Accepting Modification

"Changing one's attitude is the greatest discovery of all time because it can change one's destiny." —Oprah Winfrey.

Consider the topic of maths, which is dreaded by many. People frequently assume it's challenging and get pessimistic about it. On the other hand, people discover they can succeed when they adopt an optimistic outlook and approach arithmetic. The most important lesson is that unless you make a change, nothing will change.

If you adopt a different perspective, working remotely can become less of a drastic choice and more of an opportunity to obtain multiple rewards. Deciding whether to hire remote workers for your business, yourself, and your staff will get easier.

We all need an open and flexible mentality to handle the frequent changes that impact our lives, both favourably and negatively.

The Requirement for Modification

You must first understand why you must view the unavoidable changes positively if you want to cultivate a mindset that supports change.

Managing Change Right Now

Understanding the idea of remote work, its benefits and drawbacks, and its potential effects on your business and staff is essential to being change-ready.

Being knowledgeable can help you deal with any problems that might come up (Everything You Need to Know about the Changing World of Work, per the Economist, 2016).

Accepting Differences

Employers may access a wider range of talent through remote work, which promotes diversity in the workforce and the way they think. We must adjust and learn how to deal with these shifts as the world evolves.

Utilising Technology In today's world, Technology is a need. In the past, there was widespread concern that employment might be lost due to technological improvements. Rather,

Technology has brought about chances for development and advancement.

Imagine a revolutionary device that replaces a manual task with automation. Because of this technology, workers must acquire new skills to operate, maintain, and guarantee the quality of output rather than lose their jobs. Technology has shown itself to be more of a benefit than a danger.

The Increase in Work from Home

Although remote work has been around for a while, the COVID-19 outbreak helped to popularise it. We discovered that many duties could be completed from home and that we weren't always required to be there.

Before the pandemic, workers in creative professions like writing, design, and art had remote jobs. We all have some experience with its efficacy, so it's time to acknowledge and seize its potential.

The Great Resignation: Juggling Remote Work with Employee Needs

The Great Resignation has brought attention to the necessity of attending to the demands of employees, as individuals are more concerned than ever with their job satisfaction, work-life balance, and general well-being. Companies need to modify their approaches to attract and retain people in the wake of the COVID-19 pandemic by providing flexible work schedules and perks that accommodate a range of preferences.

For example, many workers learned the benefits of working remotely during the pandemic, including the ease of avoiding long commutes, the freedom to better manage their time, and the opportunity to achieve a better work-life balance. Employees, however, quit and looked for jobs that would offer the required perks when some employers failed to comply with their wishes.

Take Audrey's story, a marketing expert who had worked for her employer for five years. She switched to working remotely after the epidemic struck and fell in love with its flexibility.

Audrey discovered that working remotely allowed her to be more productive, spend more time with her family, and have a comfortable workspace. Nevertheless, Audrey's requests to continue working remotely were turned down when her employer switched back to in-person meetings. She quit and looked for work elsewhere when she realised she would lose the equilibrium she had discovered.

Audrey's experience during the Great Resignation was not unusual; it is representative of the experiences of many professionals. Firms must reevaluate their approaches to keep valuable personnel and consider providing remote work options, hybrid schedules, or other flexible solutions. Businesses that adapt to these developments can strengthen their teams, lower employee attrition, and maintain their competitiveness in the dynamic labour market.

Furthermore, the global integration trend—where companies cooperate with specialists worldwide—has been accelerated by the increase in remote work. Due to reduced geographical and time zone constraints, businesses can now access a large talent pool. Thanks to the globalisation of the workforce, people are now more empowered to look for jobs that fit their values and tastes without being limited by geography.

For instance, Rajnish, an Indian software developer, successfully landed a remote job with a US-based IT company. With this chance, he could pursue his passion for work in an area he was enthusiastic about and still benefits from working remotely, which included taking care of his ageing parents and striking a healthy work-life balance. John's narrative demonstrates how international integration can foster ties advantageous to businesses and employees.

Due to The Great Resignation, employees are looking for organisations that fit their needs. Global integration, flexible scheduling, and remote work are essential for businesses to retain top personnel. These elements foster a valued and empowered workforce and increase employee happiness.

The business and its employees succeed and thrive when these elements are implemented. To build a resilient and flexible future in the post-pandemic world, businesses must comprehend and adjust to the shifting terrain of employee preferences.

Chapter 5: Tracking Development and Maintaining Drive

 ensures that your attempts to increase productivity and time management are successful. Tracking your advancement towards them regularly. To help you keep organised and on schedule, you can utilise tools like calendars, time-monitoring apps, and to-do lists.

It's critical to establish SMART goals while creating them: Time-bound, relevant, quantifiable, achievable, and specific. This means you should have well-defined goals and a system to track your progress towards them. Given your existing situation and available resources, they should also be reasonable and attainable. Your goals should also have a timeframe for fulfilment and be pertinent to your overall aims.

Once your objectives have been established, it's critical to frequently assess how well you reach them. This might assist you in determining which areas could require more work or modifications. It can also sustain your motivation by giving you a distinct sense of achievement as you progress towards your objectives.

It's critical to monitor your development, acknowledge your successes, and reward yourself for your diligence. This can increase your motivation and help you stay goal-focused. Rewarding yourself can be as easy as giving yourself a nice treat or taking a break to do something you enjoy. Selecting incentives that hold significance for you and offer a feeling of fulfilment and achievement is crucial.

But it's crucial to remember that obstacles and failures are normal parts of the journey. When faced with challenges, try to maintain your positive attitude and concentrate on solving the issue rather than moping over it. Consistent, but any hurdle can be overcome with the correct attitude and strategy.

Remaining upbeat

Practising thankfulness is one method to maintain your positive attitude in the face of difficulties. Every day, set aside some time to consider your blessings, no matter how minor they may appear. This can assist you in turning your attention from the difficulties you are encountering to the things that are going well in your life.

Another motivation method is encouraging people around you who share your goals and believe in you. Talk to them about your struggles and ask for their support and guidance. Having a support system can help you stay motivated and overcome challenges.

To support your time management and productivity goals, it's crucial to establish positive habits and routines and employ tools to monitor your progress. This can involve scheduling specific time each day for concentrated work, taking regular pauses to relax and refuel, and minimising disruptions and distractions.

Engaging in mindfulness practises is one practical strategy to reduce distractions. This entails concentrating on the task and living in the present moment. You may increase your capacity for concentration and do more tasks in less time by teaching your mind to remain focused.

Setting priorities for your work and concentrating first on the most crucial ones is another technique to increase productivity. Making the most of your time and ensuring that you are moving closer to your objectives can be achieved by doing this. Methods like the Eisenhower Matrix and the ABCDE approach can assist you in setting priorities and maintaining focus on the most important things.

The ABCDE Approach

Brian Tracy invented the ABCDE approach, a potent priority-setting strategy1. It stands for A - Critical tasks that need to be completed. If these tasks are not finished, there may be dire consequences.

B) Assignments that are necessary to complete but carry little penalty if left undone.

C: Nice-to-do tasks, which don't carry any penalties if left undone.

D - Assignments that are transferable to another person.

E: Activities that can be dropped.

This method's concept is to give jobs different letters based on their importance. This makes it easier for you to decide which chores to work on yourself, which to abandon, and which to delegate to someone else.

Crucial-Urgent Matrix

The Eisenhower Matrix is an instrument for ranking tasks according to their urgency and importance, often called the Urgent-Important Matrix1. Dwight D. Eisenhower, a five-star general during World War II and the 34th President of the United States, created it.

There are four quadrants in the matrix:

1. Important and Urgent: Things that need to be done now.

2. Important but not urgent: Assignments that need to be completed now but don't have to.

3. Urgent but not Important: Unimportant tasks that don't need to be completed now.

4. Not Important nor Urgent: Unimportant tasks that don't need to be attended to now.

The purpose of the matrix is to assist you in prioritising your work by separating less important and urgent jobs that you should either delegate or not complete at all.

Effective Time Management And Psychological Well-Being

The connection between mental health and effective time management

A key component of preserving and enhancing mental health is time management skills. It has been demonstrated that being able to prioritize, plan our work, and prevent procrastination significantly affects how we feel about stress and anxiety and, consequently, how well our mental health is overall.

The modern world is chronically stressful, and feeling overworked and pressed for time are major contributors. People become more stressed when they believe they won't have enough time to complete their obligations. Chronic stress has been linked to more severe mental health issues like depression and anxiety.

By giving us a sense of control over our responsibilities and tasks, effective time management can help lower stress. Our mental health improves, and our sense of stress reduces when we believe we control our time. We may make reasonable goals for ourselves, decide how we will approach our tasks, and determine our priorities when we manage our time well.

Additionally, efficient time management might enhance our mental health by promoting a better work-life balance. Many people find it difficult to find time for personal connections, hobbies, and self-care because of their job or school obligations. However, engaging in these activities is crucial to preserving mental wellness. We may raise our quality of life and mental well-being by ensuring we devote enough time to these activities through efficient time management.

Higher self-esteem can also be a result of effective time management. We have a sense of competence and achievement when we meet our objectives and finish our work on schedule. This emotion has the power to boost our sense of self-worth and elevate our level of life happiness in general.

Conversely, procrastination frequently results in anxious, guilty, or ashamed sentiments. We may lessen these unpleasant emotions and enhance our mental well-being through efficient time management and avoiding procrastination.

And last, effective time management can promote increased mental toughness. Effective time management helps us become better at handling stress and failures. This may improve our capacity to handle stress and adjust to challenging circumstances, which is essential for maintaining mental health. Thus, time management skills can be important for preserving and enhancing our mental health. Effective time management can improve mental health and quality of life by lowering stress, promoting a better work-life balance, boosting self-esteem, decreasing procrastination, and building greater resilience.

Have a big impact on our mental health, even while it isn't a panacea for all mental health problems. We can enhance our quality of life and mental health by improving time management. But it's also critical to keep in mind that mental health is complex and may call for a range of therapeutic modalities, such as counselling, medication, and self-care. Effective time management is but one aspect of the mental health puzzle.

How better time management might enhance mental well-being

A condition of emotional, cognitive, and social well-being, but also a crucial aspect of overall health. Effective time management has been shown to have a substantial positive impact on mental health.

Being able to manage your time well can help prevent stress, anxiety, and other mental health issues in today's busy and fast-paced environment when we confront many difficulties and demands. Time management techniques allow for creating balanced and controlled daily routines that improve an individual's environment.

First of all, stress can be reduced by efficient time management. When we manage our time well, we can complete our tasks and commitments on time and to the best of our abilities. We reduce our stress by avoiding the last-minute hurry and the sensation of being overburdened. Furthermore, having a well-planned and organized schedule allows us to feel certain that we are headed in the right direction toward our objectives.

Time management reduces stress and enhances work-life balance, which is important for mental health. We can create work and personal time boundaries by identifying and prioritizing our tasks. This enables us to allocate meaningful time to leisure pursuits, interpersonal interactions, and self-care—all essential mental health components.

Furthermore, time management skills might help us feel more responsible for our lives. Our self-esteem and sense of competence increase when we believe we are in charge of our lives and are not just responding to outside circumstances. Since we feel more capable and confident in our ability to handle events, this improved self-confidence.

Through a positive outlook, time management can also enhance mental health. We may observe progress and achievement when we have a clear action plan, set reasonable targets, and then meet them. These, in turn, boost our drive and provide us with a feeling of contentment and fulfilment, all of which help us have a more optimistic view of life.

Effective time management enables us to set aside time for pursuits like physical activity, meditation, or just unwinding that directly improve our mental health. Each of these pursuits has been shown to improve mental health, and effective time management guarantees that we can fit them into our daily schedules.

But it's crucial to keep in mind that not all mental health issues can be solved by time management. It is not a replacement for getting professional assistance when coping with a major mental illness, even while it can help create a better environment and lower certain risk factors. Still, efficient time management can play a major role in a thorough and proactive strategy to preserve and enhance our mental health. By lowering stress, enhancing work-life balance, boosting self-assurance, encouraging positivity, and enabling the inclusion of mentally beneficial activities in daily life, time management can assist in promoting mental health. As usual, to ensure that time management techniques are both successful and long-lasting, we must customize them to meet our own demands and circumstances. We may utilize time management as a potent tool to enhance our mental health if we consistently practice and commit to it.

Second Pillar: Use Your Energy

You might be shocked to learn how many factors affect your energy levels. These include your stress levels, emotions, food, and exercise regimen. Time management is vital, but so is energy management. Everything you do requires energy investment, including thoughts, behaviours, emotions, and tasks. As a result, the energy you devote to a work should correspond with it.

You need mental, emotional, and physical energy to accomplish tasks you take on and want to finish with all your attention. Since energy must be renewed, it is not an endless spring. You must balance using and replenishing your energy because too much or too little will deplete it. You can store more energy. Consider athletes: to improve, they work hard in the gym and push themselves to the limit. When it comes to energy, the same is true. Exert as much energy as you can during practice, but I strongly advise against going beyond. Nobody is more aware of your boundaries than you.

You may maximize your energy capacity by employing routines to increase and control your available energy. Your energy capacity is a component of who you are that requires maintenance, much like your health.

The Dilemma of Dieting

You will notice fluctuations in your energy levels throughout the day. This is an inevitable frequent event, like breakfast, lunch, and midday snacks. However, be advised that not all foods will increase your energy levels or won't last long. Certain foods deplete energy, making you feel sluggish and unable to focus.

Even if we usually realize consuming something is not a good idea, we do it. This is a result of the reward system in our brains. Some contend that eating a few doughnuts and a cup of coffee tastes far better than consuming a nutritious breakfast. A common misconception is that nutritious food doesn't taste nice. However, look around you; there are many recipe books full of delicious, affordable, and healthful breakfast and lunch options that can help you feel more energized throughout the day. What do you think? Do you eat wholesome foods or just whatever is on hand?

Hack 12: Steer clear of foods and beverages that deplete energy!

These are the meals and beverages you should stay away from if you want to have a day full of energy and productivity:

Take It Easy With Cuppa Joe

Coffee is not inherently unhealthy, so stop worrying. Coffee consumption in moderation can benefit one's physical and mental health. For a brief period, caffeine will increase your energy and cognitive function. Excessive coffee consumption leads to body resistance, which reduces efficiency.

Items Added with Sugar

These days, many food products—like yoghurt and morning cereals—are sold with added sugar. Does eating these make you feel good? It does, but only because it sets off a reaction in your brain that immediately makes you feel satisfied. An energy surge is produced by a jump in your blood sugar levels, but this energy quickly wanes, leading to a sugar crash. Even though you had a nice and sweet breakfast, you'll be wondering why you're so exhausted and unable to concentrate as soon as you get to the office.

Low-Calorie Foods

While some may take pride in maintaining a low-calorie diet, doing so may eventually harm their health. Every day, your body requires a specific quantity of calories, even for fundamental processes like breathing and heartbeat. You could run out of energy if you consume too few calories. You'll feel exhausted and find concentrating difficult when your metabolism slows down.

Grain Processing

Grains can provide a lot of energy because they are abundant in carbs. On the other hand, eating foods high in processed carbohydrates, such as white bread and rice, could lower your energy levels. This is because the outer layer that contained fibre has been removed, accelerating the rate at which the food is absorbed. These foods might provide a short-term energy boost, but your blood sugar and energy levels will decrease quickly, causing a sugar crash.

Quick Eats

It is much simpler to buy fast or fried food for lunch because most people just have an hour or so. It's delicious, quick, and simple. There is more to eating fast food than knowing it is unhealthy and might make us gain weight. Due to its high fat content and low fibre content, it is rapidly digested and doesn't supply much energy. Fast food or deep-fried foods typically lack significant amounts of essential elements, like vitamins and minerals.

Energy Liquids

Because energy drinks typically have significant caffeine content, your body may grow accustomed to their effects. Although the feeling of having a lot more energy is fleeting, it can be attributed to the high sugar content of energy drinks. You get that sugar high all over again, but then there's a drop.

Hack 13: Foods and Drinks That Boost Energy: Savor them!

Let's examine foods and beverages that boost your energy, concentration, and productivity.

B-complex vitamins

Put another way, eating foods high in this vitamin can make you feel happier, which could increase energy and productivity. Changing things up can only be beneficial because being in a poor mood may be exhausting. Foods high in vitamin B include meat, eggs, broccoli, pecans, peas, spinach, and whole grains.

Sip Water

During the night, your body consumes a lot of water for chemical processes like cell repair. For this reason, as soon as you wake up, you should drink a glass of water. Consume adequate water to maintain your energy levels since dehydration can cause you to lose focus and productivity.

antioxidants

touch with substances that are bad for your health, like tobacco smoke.

Antioxidants shield your cells from harmful free radicals, promoting overall wellness. Antioxidant-rich meals, on the other hand, also support cognitive performance. Blueberries, strawberries, and raspberries are some of these foods.

Fatty Acids Omega-3

By controlling blood sugar, lowering inflammation, creating new brain cells, and mending and rebuilding brain cell membranes, omega-3 fatty acids support brain function. It also elevates your mood and enhances memory and focus. Omega-3 fatty acids even fight off depression and dementia. It contains foods including salmon, kale, eggs, avocados, flaxseeds, and wild game.

Complete Protein

Protein keeps you fuller for longer than most other nutrients; did you know that? You become more focused, aware, and awake, increasing your productivity. Protein-rich foods include meat, beans, fish, nuts, and eggs. Protein is usually an excellent idea when it comes to breakfast.

Lutein

Strong antioxidant lutein reduces the deterioration of cognitive function. Additionally, it fights conditions in the eyes, like cataracts and age-related macular degeneration. Thus, incorporate some broccoli, spinach, lettuce, kale, or egg yolks into your diet to keep your mind active and focused.

Divide Up The Work Into Doable Parts

3.1 The Advantages of Dividing Up Work

You may easily handle even the most difficult jobs by using a time management strategy that involves dividing activities into smaller, more manageable portions. You may simplify difficult jobs, sharpen your attention, and keep moving toward your objectives by breaking things up into smaller components. The following are some advantages of task division:

1. Overcome procrastination: Overwhelming large or complex chores often cause people to put them off. Tasks feel less overwhelming when broken

down into smaller, more manageable chunks, which enables you to get beyond resistance and take the initial step.

2. Boost productivity and focus: Concentrating on and finishing smaller activities is simpler, increasing output. Your drive to keep working toward your goal will be fueled by the achievement you get from finishing each task.

3. Effective time management involves breaking up work into smaller segments so that you may use your time more wisely. Smaller chores are easier to fit into your schedule, and you might even be able to finish some of them during quick breaks or idle moments.

4. Track progress: Keeping tabs on your development and assessing your

performance when activities are broken down is simpler. Off minor tasks as you accomplish them.

5. Identify and prioritize a project's more vital or time-sensitive components more easily by breaking tasks down into smaller segments. You can more efficiently manage your time and resources by doing this.

6. Decrease emotions of tension and overload: Dividing work into manageable portions can assist in lowering the stress and overwhelm that comes with taking on big or complicated undertakings. Your confidence will increase as you finish each little task, and the project as a whole will become easier to handle.

7. Encourage teamwork: Dividing work into manageable chunks simplifies assigning and coordinating tasks in a group. Team members find it easier to comprehend their roles and how their efforts fit into the bigger picture of the project.

The upcoming sub-chapters will cover the many methods for dividing activities into manageable portions and how to successfully incorporate this strategy into your time management plan.

A. Recognizing the significance of time management

Success in both the personal and professional spheres depends on having a solid understanding of time management. The practice of efficiently planning, arranging, and allocating time to fulfil the needs of your daily duties and long-term objectives is known as time management.

Consider, for instance, that you are a professional who works from 9 to 5 and has a family to support. You must efficiently manage your time to take care of your family, finish your work on time, and have some free time. If you don't manage your time well, you can find it difficult to fulfil work obligations, overlook your family's needs, and experience stress and overwhelmed.

However, if you have good time management skills, you can plan your days to manage your personal and professional lives. You may arrange your projects into priority lists, assign deadlines, and make sure you finish the most crucial assignments first. Be more productive, whether it involves finishing a significant project at work or spending more time with your family.

Effective time management also makes the most of your time and taking charge of your life possible. Setting priorities and concentrating on the most crucial tasks helps you avoid becoming sidetracked by urgent or unnecessary work. Additionally, you can employ time management strategies to maximize your free time, lower stress levels, and boost productivity.

Being more productive is one of the main advantages of time management. You can do more in a day when you have good time management skills since you can finish more chores in less time. You can achieve more of your goals and objectives, which can help you succeed in both your personal and professional life.

Managing your time well also helps you feel better overall and reduces stress. When you create and follow a time management plan, you can feel more in control of your life and less stressed by your everyday obligations. This may make you feel happier and more at ease.

Moreover, time management skills help you establish a more favourable work-life balance. You may lead a balanced and satisfying life when you are good at managing your time so that you have time for both your personal and professional lives.

You can boost your general wellbeing, become more productive, and lessen stress with effective time management. You can take charge of your life and maximize your time by realizing the significance of time management.

Chapter Eleven

Break the Chain: Become more determined and driven.

Lack of enthusiasm and willpower is a common cause of procrastination. This chapter examines the intricate relationships between motivation and willpower as well as the psychological influences on them. Take a deep dive into motivational and willpower-building techniques to learn how to break free from the chains of procrastination and move toward constant, productive action.

The Myth of Willpower: Comprehending the Absence of Ego

Even if willpower is sometimes seen as an endless resource, it can run out of ego. You can control your willpower more successfully if you know its limitations.

Depletion of ego

Following decision-making or self-control exercises in earlier activities, a decrease in self-control and willpower is called "ego depletion." This phenomenon emphasizes how willpower is a limited resource that can easily run out.

Fatigue with decisions

Making many decisions throughout the day can lead to decision fatigue, which impairs your capacity to make deliberate judgments and avoid temptation. Recognizing when you become weary of making decisions enables you to strategically use your little willpower.

Increasing Willpower Through Muscle Training in Self-Discipline

Consistent exercise and conscious effort can increase willpower, a mental muscle. Putting self-discipline improvement techniques into practice makes it easier for you to overcome procrastination.

Establish a cornerstone habit.

As previously mentioned, fundamental behaviours greatly influence all facets of life. You may increase your resilience and willpower by forming crucial habits that enhance self-discipline.

Establish little tasks.

Take up daily challenges that call for self-control, like getting up early or finishing a certain task without becoming sidetracked. Your willpower will be exercised as these difficulties get harder.

Motivational Test: Distinguishing Between Internal and External Elements

Motivation is complex and influenced by both internal and external variables. Using dynamics successfully requires an understanding of how these components interact.

Motivation from within

Internal elements, including self-interest, enthusiasm, and a sense of achievement, are the source of intrinsic motivation. Developing projects aligned with your interests and values will increase intrinsic motivation and make procrastination less appealing.

Outside Insight

Extrinsic motivation stems from incentives or outcomes from outside sources, including praise or penalties. While it may work well in the near term, relying only on outside motivation over time may result in burnout and a decline in engagement.

Myths about Motivation: The Incentives for Taking Action

The action frequently comes before motive, despite what the public believes. Even if you're not motivated, working on activities might start a positive feedback loop that makes you motivated.

Loop of motivation-action

Even in the absence of incentive, action starts a feedback loop. You feel accomplished and make progress when you finish a task, and this gives you the drive to continue.

Dynamic Zeigarnik Effect

Motivation is impacted by the Zeigarnik effect, previously explored in task completion. Beginning a task causes psychological tension, encouraging you to finish it and increasing motivation.

Engage in mindfulness meditation to enhance concentration and lower anxiety.

The age-old practice of mindfulness meditation has been well-known in recent years due to its many advantages, which include its ability to increase focus, lower stress levels, and improve general wellbeing. In a time when there are a lot of distractions and demands on our time, mindfulness meditation can be a useful tool for developing a more tranquil, productive, and focused mindset.

Fundamentally, mindfulness meditation brings an open, curious, and accepting attitude while focusing on the present moment. You train your mind to be present and give your whole attention to whatever you're feeling instead of dwelling on regrets from the past or worries about the future. This could include your breathing, your body's feelings, thoughts, emotions, or even the sights and noises around you.

The ability to control where your attention is focused and becoming more aware of where it is are two important ways mindfulness meditation can help you become more focused. You effectively perform a "rep" of attentional training each time you catch your mind straying during meditation—which it certainly will—and gently bring it back to your selected focus. Practising can help you become more focused and able to block out distractions during meditation and your day-to-day activities and professional endeavours.

Through the encouragement of a more accepting and nonjudgmental attitude toward your experiences, mindfulness meditation can also aid in stress reduction. Stress is frequently made worse by our responses to upsetting situations or feelings. You can make room to select more deliberate and stress-free reactions by learning to watch these events without jumping to conclusions. Furthermore, it has been discovered that practising mindfulness meditation increases activity in brain regions linked to attention and emotional regulation while decreasing activity stress and terror responses.

It is quite simple to practice mindfulness meditation, and no special tools are needed. Allot a brief daily period in a calm and cosy location. Shut your eyes and focus on your breathing, observing its sensation as it enters and exits your body. You will inevitably find your thoughts wandering. When it does, gently and nonjudgmentally bring it back to your breath. As your attention increases with practice, you can progressively lengthen your meditation periods.

Many materials are available to assist you in beginning mindfulness meditation, such as books, courses, apps, and guided meditations. The most crucial aspect is to practice mindfulness meditation regularly, though, as its advantages tend to compound and become more profound over time.

In summary, mindfulness meditation is effective for raising focus and lowering stress. Your ability to stay calm, focused, and resilient can greatly improve your productivity and general quality of life. You can teach your mind to stay present and respond less automatically to stimuli.

Being on time is crucial for fostering positive relationships with other people.

Being on time is vital to fostering relationships with people, whether for a job interview, a crucial meeting, or just a get-together. Being punctual demonstrates your respect for the other person and your appreciation for their time. This increases the likelihood that they will regard you as dependable, which is always positive!

Try being more on time if your tardiness has upset other people in your life, even if it involves getting up earlier than normal!

Being on time is crucial for a variety of reasons. It first demonstrates your regard for other people's time just as much as yours. When someone is late, cancels on you, or puts off doing something at the last minute, it's impossible not to become irritated. You'll lead by example and encourage others to follow your lead by being punctual.

Second, it's simpler to establish friends when you arrive on time in social circumstances! That's exactly what I want people to think of me when they meet me early: "Oh wow this person is so nice! They came early so we could talk more before the event started." It makes me more approachable and helps people form opinions about me before they even know my name (which has happened). What's the fastest way to accomplish this? Arrive early!

Finally, and perhaps most crucially, being on time demonstrates to others that we are trustworthy individuals who will honour our commitments and not abandon them at the last minute. This will make things easier later on when we collaborate on projects because everyone knows that we always—or at least attempt to—show up when we say we will.

Being consistently late makes life more difficult and busy.

Being late all the time makes it hard to be punctual and organized. It not only makes things harder for you, but it also makes things harder for everyone else around you.

When you arrive late, other people must rearrange their schedules to accommodate you. They can't go about their day and get things done that they need to get done till they wait for you. They may become angry and frustrated with you or others who depend on you for promptness (such as family members).

Since there will be less time in a day or week for any work that takes longer than anticipated, it might also be stressful for you . If you arrive late for a task and take twice as long as expected, a significant portion of your leisure time will be spent finishing this incomplete work, which is not how we want to spend our lives! Rather than pushing ourselves into exhaustion trying to keep up with everything on our plate, we would rather spend our lives having fun with friends and family.

Being on time can help you land a job.

Being on time can make you more employable. Hiring is based on a candidate's dependability, responsibility, and punctuality; if you arrive to interviews late or unprepared, your chances of getting hired are low.

Additionally, you don't want to irritate people by consistently being late. People get frustrated when you're late, and it might also make them think less of you and your dependability. If your delay causes your coworkers or bosses to think ill of you, it may be more difficult for you to get along with them.

Punctuality Encourages Mental Wellness

One of the most crucial things you can do for your emotional wellbeing is to be on time. Others find it difficult to organize their days when they are late or miss meetings and appointments, which hurts their mental health. If you are late for everything and cause people inconvenience, they can get resentful of you or stop inviting you to activities entirely.

Honouring others and yourself by being punctual. People who rely on one another's schedules may experience unnecessary stress from being late, which may result in health issues like heart attacks and strokes as well as subpar performance at work or school! Always try to appear on time, or even a bit early, to prevent unnecessary stress in other people's lives.

Being on time is crucial in life. Your coworkers may become resentful of you if you arrive late to work and believe you don't care about the current project. The person who organized the appointment might think you don't value their time if you are late. In any scenario, punctuality will guarantee that everyone has faith in your skills and commitment to the task.

Handling Diversion

Distractions have the power to steal our focus and undermine time management. Techniques for overcoming distractions:

Establish a Space Free from Distractions: Reduce the amount of distractions in your workspace by shutting off pointless notifications on your computer or phone and locating a quiet area where you can concentrate.

Employ a Time Lock: Establish time slots for distinct work and ensure you do not interfere during these intervals. Inform folks in your vicinity that you are not available at these times.

Exercise Self-Control: Gain the capacity to concentrate and refocus your attention when distracted.

Acquire the ability to recognise instances of distraction and employ strategies to regain concentration.

Maintaining Motivation

When it comes to managing your time, motivation is essential.

Several strategies for maintaining motivation include:

Make Ambitious Goals: Make sure your goals are motivating and significant to you.

Verify if these objectives reflect your values and aspirations.

Honour minor victories:

Acknowledge and commemorate your incremental successes, regardless of their magnitude.

This gives you more confidence and keeps you motivated.

Locate Inspirational Sources: Look for motivation in books, articles, films, or others discussing goal-achieving techniques and success stories.

Acquiring Knowledge from Difficulties

One step in the time management process is overcoming obstacles.

Take what you can from their struggles and experiences, pinpoint areas that need work, and modify your approach accordingly.

I hope this chapter has given you the motivation and strength to persevere through obstacles on your time management path.

Struggling and maintaining focus on your objectives is critical despite any roadblocks.

Remember that every person is different, so you might need to modify these strategies to fit your needs and preferences.

Utilising the Pareto Principle (80/20 Rule)

The 80/20 rule, sometimes called the Pareto Principle, is a productivity and efficiency tactic frequently applied in corporate and personal growth. This means that around 80% of effects are caused by 20% of causes. This idea may be used for several things, such as goal-setting, time management, decision-making, etc.

Applying the 80/20 approach to time management is crucial to achieving your objectives and eliminating or assigning time-consuming jobs requiring unnecessary effort. You may increase productivity and produce better results by concentrating on the 20% of tasks with the biggest impact.

1. Determine which jobs are most crucial: Decide which of your duties is the most crucial and will affect your objectives the most. Your primary focus should be on these tasks.

2. Remove or assign non-essential duties: Remove or assign tasks that don't advance your objectives or aren't necessary. Time saved for other crucial duties will result from this.

3. Concentrate on high-value tasks: Give your time and attention to high-value ones with a greater chance of producing noteworthy outcomes.

4. Review and change frequently: Review and adjust your tasks regularly to ensure you are still concentrating on the most crucial jobs and moving closer to your objectives.

For instance, if you work in sales, you might discover that 20% of your clients account for 80% of your revenue. Your productivity will rise, and your sales will be optimised if you can pinpoint these high-value clients and focus on them.

Benefits of time management with the 80/20 rule:

1. Prioritisation: The 80/20 rule assists you in setting priorities for your work and concentrating on the most crucial tasks that advance your objectives. Concentrating on the most important tasks will help you work more efficiently and provide better outcomes.

2. Time-saving: You can save time and energy for more critical duties by recognising, removing, or assigning non-essential tasks. You may be able to operate more efficiently and swiftly as a result.

3. Better decision-making: By concentrating on the most important elements that support your objectives, the 80/20 rule assists you in making better judgements. You can improve your decision-making and outcome by concentrating on the 20% of variables that matter most.

4. Increased productivity: You may increase your concentration on the most important activities, eliminating unnecessary ones and learning to work more efficiently.

For instance, if you are a software engineer, you may discover that 20% of the codebase is responsible for 80% of the defects in your code. You may increase productivity and produce software of higher calibre by recognising and concentrating on the crucial codebase areas that influence issue fixes. In summary, you may prioritise your work, save time, make better decisions, and increase productivity using the 80/20 rule in time management. You may accomplish your goals more rapidly and successfully if you learn to prioritise your chores and work more efficiently.

Increasing Levels of Motivation and Energy

Increasing drive and vigour is a crucial component of efficient time management. You can concentrate better, work more productively, and complete more tasks in less time when your energy and motivation levels are high. The following are some strategies to raise your motivation and energy levels:

1. Engage in regular exercise: Regular exercise can boost your motivation and energy levels. Natural mood enhancers called endorphins are released during exercise. A quick workout might help you feel more energised and be more productive.

2. Consume a balanced diet: protein will give you greater energy all day. Sugary, processed foods should be avoided as they can create energy dumps.

4. Get enough sleep: Sleep deprivation can cause low mood and diminished motivation. Ensure you receive enough

sleep each night to have a wakeful and productive day.

5. Engage in constructive self-talk: This might help you become more motivated and confident. Goal-focused by taking the place of negative thoughts in your mind.

6. Establish attainable goals: Achievable goals will keep you engaged and task-focused. To simplify bigger goals, break them down into smaller, more doable tasks.

What Makes a Difference?

Why, then, can working from home instead of an office boost productivity? Let's examine some key elements that increase productivity at home in more detail.

Reduction in Travel Time

No matter how long your commute is in the morning and evening, it still determines the course of your day. You'll likely arrive at work exhausted and agitated if caught in early morning traffic. You won't likely be in the best of moods when you get home if the same thing occurs on the way there. Daily commutes are eliminated when working from home. First, since they won't need to travel, employees can begin work on schedule or early.

Furthermore, workers will start their workdays with more energy and a positive attitude. Last but not least, less travel means a better environment. You can reduce your carbon impact by utilising your automobile or public transportation less.

Fewer Things to Stress Over

It feels wonderful to cross something off our to-do list when we have such hectic lifestyles. Imagine not needing to wake up early to get enough time to apply cosmetics or iron your clothes. These are not as big of a concern when you work from home. In addition, there are things like making it to your child's concert or stopping at the petrol station in the evening to avoid being late in the morning. You get a clearer schedule and a less busy mind when you eliminate the rush of travel time and irritated coworkers who won't let you work and work out when to fit in your workout. Less worries free up your thinking and make it easier to develop ideas. This has a profound impact on how you operate.

Improved Harmony between Work and Life

A clear work/life balance is possible if you work from home and set clear boundaries. You'll be able to find more time to work out, explore new interests, and spend more time with your loved ones. All of this helps you live a more balanced life rather than one where work takes up all of your energy.

Reduced Interruptions

It is simpler to become sidetracked or interrupted from work when you are at an office. Coworkers may be chatting loudly to one another, that they want to show you their new cat, or that you get sucked into a discussion about last night's football game. This reduces the time you can spend working and makes it harder to return to the flow state you were in before being interrupted. It may also be difficult for you to call clients; in this case, you must choose a quiet meeting space or go outside. Making phone calls is simpler, and these noisy distractions are eliminated when working from home.

Adaptable Timetable

You can have a flexible schedule if you work from home and use your time well. Supervisors typically don't mind if staff members leave for a meeting or pick up students from school as long as they can effectively manage their time and remain productive. This allows you extra time to complete tasks that you would typically try to fit into your weekends or assign to others. I've discovered that I can even work remotely while on the road with the right time management.

Pros and Cons of the Productivity-Based Team Approach

A team may stay informed and ensure activities are finished on time using team-based productivity tools. But, depending on the size of your company, it may be expensive, and the initial setup will take some time.

That concludes the programmes and administrative techniques you can use to organise your virtual office. Recall that having the appropriate tools may help you work well in any environment, regardless of where you set up your workspace. This will provide you with a strong base to continue being productive. The next thing to do is figure out how to work from home without becoming distracted.

www.ingramcontent.com/pod-product-compliance
Lightning Source LLC
Chambersburg PA
CBHW052134110526
44591CB00012B/1715